Unleashing the Power of Pervasive Leadership

A THREE SEVEN RESEARCH, INC. KEY CONCEPT SUMMARY

PERVASIVE LEADERSHIP RECOGNIZES THAT EACH OF US SHOULD BE A LEADER INDEPENDENT OF OUR TITLE OR POSITION. EACH OF US HAS A KEY ROLE IN CREATING THE FUTURE WE DESIRE – A GREAT FUTURE.

First Edition: November 2014
ISBN : 978-0692229705

Three-Seven Research, Inc. Publishing
www.threesevenresearch.com
1 Sea Marsh Rd
Amelia Island Fl, 32034

Print and e-book version available at
Amazon.com

CONTENTS

WHY ANOTHER LEADERSHIP BOOK?

The market is flooded with leadership books - literally thousands of titles crying for your attention. Why, then, should you select this one? After all, it's shorter than most (perhaps that is actually a reason to read it) and not written by a celebrity. It does not promise instant wealth or success.

Yet, the concept is intriguing - "Pervasive Leadership". What does this imply? Is it to be confused with "perverse leadership"? Does it imply that leadership should be dispersed with everyone free to determine the organization's policy and direction? Or is it a liberating concept - one that frees the human spirit to excel and create a far better future?

Indeed, it's the latter. "Pervasive Leadership" highlights the sweet spot in the leadership continuum occupying a position well between the dictator and the lazy, absent leader. It recognizes that the role of a true leader is to set the course, provide needed resources, establish a positive culture and gain the commitment of the entire team to accomplish their goals. It recognizes that mature leaders understand their role and relax control in the belief that a better product will be provided and, with it, a new generation of leaders will emerge.

A second reason for considering this short book is its relevant, performance based approach. Pervasive Leadership is built around Three-Seven Research's hallmark 'Seven Characteristics of Successful Organizations'. Combining these seven organizational principles with the magic of pervasive leadership provides the basis for organizational renewal and sustainable success.

Lastly, these concepts are actionable. The "Seven Characteristics" and pervasive leadership concepts were developed over decades of real life - conceived in failure, refined in success. The focus is on practical application, not esoteric theory. Each chapter includes exercises to assist you understand and apply the principles - no matter what your title or position on the antiquated organizational chart.

In summary, this book encourages you to apply advanced leadership concepts with time proven approaches to increase your personal and organizational success. Join us on this journey - it has the power to transform your life as it has ours!

Seven Characteristics of Successful Organizations

1. **Clarity of Purpose** – a clear and compelling reason for existing, a goal worthy of our best effort.

2. **Intuitive, Effective Processes** – consistent, efficient methods for achieving our goals that properly balance the use of technology and individual skills.

3. **Exceptional Teamwork** – people with the right skills and attitudes working together.

4. **Commitment to Organizational Success** – individual and corporate ownership for achieving our common goals.

5. **Innovation and Renewal** – a willingness to try new approaches and encourage fresh ideas.

6. **Energizing, Encouraging Culture** – respectful, supportive and solution oriented.

7. **Pervasive Leadership** – people throughout the organization actively working to develop each of the first six attributes.

I
WHAT LEADERS DO

Clearly defining the leader's roles compels others to join their ranks

It was a time of severe challenge. It was not just individuals that were failing, but the very organization! If we were to retain our livelihood and our company, change was imperative.

But where should we start? Our product, electricity, was fundamental to society and our technology proven in hundreds of locations throughout the world. Our people had been successful in the past, being recognized as industry leaders a mere decade before.

In the end, the critical change that lead to the organization's resurgence was renewal of leadership. First we defined the unique leadership roles in positive, forward looking terms. Only then were we able to identify and develop individuals to fill these roles. The transformation, both in performance and job satisfaction, came when we realized that leadership is not limited to certain individuals by virtue of their position, but needs to be broadly shared throughout the organization.

This is the story of our journey – a journey conceived in chaos, tested by crisis and rewarded with success. It is the story of common people who, with courage, commitment and purpose, exchanged that crisis for the elation of victory. Yet, the journey is not over, for true success is continually redefined, its standards raised and its rewards expanded.

Our journey started with the simple recognition of what true leaders do rather defining them in terms of organizational charts. Our simple explanation of leadership is found in the following principles:

Leaders create the future

- Leaders define the organization's vision, providing a clear purpose.

- They bring the vision to life, compelling and empowering teams to make it a reality.

- They set expectations by presenting a clear picture of both the goal and process for its achievement.

- They define success in meaningful, measurable terms.

- They motivate, generate energy and create an environment for action.

Leaders actively develop a positive culture

- Leaders develop and practice a culture of respect and trust where each individual commits their unique and significant talents to achieve excellence.

- They engage themselves and their team by looking ahead to anticipate future needs and resolving issues before they become a crisis.

- They set an example, remaining true to their core values of integrity, respect and optimism.

- They are committed to the organization and they expect the same from their team.

Do you see yourself in these descriptions? Do you long to make a difference - to be part of a winning team? Dreaming big dreams is a start, as is defining leaders by what they do instead of their title.

Leaders deliver exceptional results

- Leaders break down barriers and provide support to achieve the near-term goals needed to realize the long-term purpose.

- They are an active part of the team, sharing in its challenges and successes.

- They are accountable, asking "Did we accomplish what we set out to do?"

- They develop the team by encouraging collaboration and inspiring commitment.

Yet, there is more. The next step is that of personal commitment - transitioning from abstract philosophy to specific actions. It requires a change from general "third-person" statements to "first-person" commitments to your organization.

As a Leader, I am personally committed to sustained excellence

I am passionate and personally committed. I invest myself in creating a culture where we grow and our team has the resources to accomplish goals previously viewed as impossible. To achieve this, my principles – the commitments I make to myself and to those around me – include:

- Entrusting my heart to our vision and our people, because if I don't, then there is no reason for me to take a stand. I ask you to display the same courage so we can succeed.

- Creating energy through a positive, forward-looking attitude and a shared understanding of the importance of achieving our vision.

- Establishing challenging goals with clear expectations that demand action to get results.

- Building an environment that encourages innovation, trusts individual talents, respects differences, develops skills and nurtures collaboration so that you will take initiative and empower yourself.

- Recognizing that individual empowerment requires personal responsibility for achieving the organization's goals while meeting high standards of integrity. The freedom associated with empowerment leads us to higher performance standards.

- Committing to excellence through continuous improvement. Embracing the fact that knowledge comes from celebrating successes and learning from failures. I understand and appreciate that 'excellence' is a dynamic concept that never rests.

- Engaging myself and expecting the engagement of those around me. We can succeed only if everyone gives their best.

- Proving myself through my actions. I will cultivate you by letting you join in my successes and failures to encourage your leadership development.

- Believing that, together, we can change the world – making it a better place for all.

Will you join me in this quest for meaning and accomplishment? That is the purpose of this book! How are we going to change our world?

Application: What Leaders Do

With any successful endeavor, active involvement is required. Likewise, each step in our leadership journey requires our personal understanding, application and commitment. Each chapter includes a few actions designed to achieve these goals. We encourage you to actively pursue them for the rewards are great!

There are many approaches to gaining value from the applications. For example, use a journal to actively write responses to the applications and reflect on the insights you gain through their application. Update your journal as you gain experience and insight. You will be encouraged as you live the applications and see the changes in your leadership success.

Let's start by reflecting on what leaders do:

1. Reflect on someone you admire, someone who "gets things done" while encouraging those who do the actual work. How do they model the roles of leaders summarized in this chapter?

2. For one week, seek to support two people in leadership roles by encouraging them. Actively listen to their ideas and provide positive feedback without explaining how they could do better. Volunteer to assist them in realistic, practical ways and then follow through on your commitment.

3. Reflect on how the leaders reacted to your involvement. How does this experience shape your view of a leader's role?

"Give instruction to a wise man and he will be still wiser; Teach a just man and he will increase in learning."

Proverbs 9:9 NKJV[i]

II
A LEADERSHIP CRISIS

Our organization, our society, is crying out for true leaders!

It was a bad day – a necessary but delayed acceptance that we were unsuccessful. Our failure was obvious to all, costing the company millions of dollars and losing the respect of several stakeholders. If it had been a football game we would have lost 53 to 10. Instead of learning from defeat, we were busy justifying our failure. The offense was happy to have scored 10 – if only the defense had stopped the opponent's long plays. The defense accepted that their performance was not outstanding, but the offense should have scored and if they would have not fumbled three times, inside the ten yard line, we would have had a chance. We longed to return to a decade earlier when we were the undisputed champions – the ones others desired to emulate.

But it was not a football game. It was our livelihood. We were unreliable and too expensive. We were out of options – we had to either improve our performance or fade into oblivion with other great

American icons like Circuit City, Lehman Brothers, Pontiac, Pan Am, Bethlehem Steel, and a host of others.

What was our underlying problem? How could our well known company have periods of glory followed by organization-threatening poor performance? The people doing the actual work had not changed dramatically – many had been with the company for twenty years or more. There were no major labor disputes, there was no new technology trying to put us out of business. Yes, the machinery was getting older and the regulations more complex, but those were not the fundamental problem.

Leadership? Could ineffective leadership be inhibiting our performance? We were like a football team without someone calling the plays, a team where each player did what they felt best without considering whether it was a run, pass or punt. In hindsight it was predictable that chaos would ensue.

Yes. We lacked true leadership. Each work group was struggling to achieve their self-defined goals. There was little coordination among groups, little consideration of what could go wrong and developing options for resolving problems instead of pushing them to another work group. Operations could always defer to poor maintenance who, in turn, could defer to inadequate engineering or planning since their job was to "fix" things not design them or ensure that all needed parts were available. Respect and trust were not to be found.

Leadership, at all levels, was needed to solve this – to get us back into the game. We started by looking at ourselves. We asked critical questions, individually and as a group, concerning what needed to change. We asked people throughout the organization whether we had the capability for success. Did we understand our business? Did we have the required skills and tools? In the end, it was not a matter of capability, but of commitment to common goals. The fundamental role of leaders in establishing a common purpose, demonstrating commitment and developing trust were absent.

We started a journey together, drawing from our experience – from those times that we were successful. We learned from others in our industry and other industries with sustained high performance.

Within a year our performance turned around – not in a slow, evolutionary way but in a transformational way. Nearly all objective performance measures improved by tens of percentage points and our profitability tripled. More importantly, it became a fun place to work again. We celebrated successes together and, as a team, worked to resolve challenges.

What changed? Leadership!

No, it was not a new group of managers that came in to "fix" the workforce. There was not a new star quarterback or point guard that energized the team with heroic feats. There was no field marshal to rally the troops or great orator to tickle the ears with fine sounding theories.

Pervasive Leadership: The change came because many people throughout the organization chose to lead rather than be spectators or victims.

It was true leadership – the understanding of what needed to be done, of seeing the broader picture and understanding each group's and individual's unique role in achieving it. It was leadership throughout the organization reaching across departmental boundaries to identify the underlying issues and jointly working to resolve them. It was through leadership of those closest to the work, who saw the process weaknesses and their supervisors who had the authority to make needed changes. It was senior leaders who helped establish a positive culture of respect and commitment. The change came because many people throughout the organization chose to lead instead of being spectators or victims.

Sustainable success came when leadership was expressed throughout the organization at all levels, in all groups. There was energy, purpose and commitment where apathy previously prevailed. Our processes became more efficient, respecting the uniqueness of individuals and eliminating the multitude of administrative barriers that previously prevailed.

As we continued to learn with the intent of continuing to improve, we found success was linked to seven characteristics:

Seven Characteristics of Successful Organizations

1. **Clarity of Purpose** – a clear and compelling reason for existing, a goal worthy of our best effort.

2. **Intuitive, Effective Processes** – consistent, efficient methods for achieving our goals that properly balance the use of technology and individual skills.

3. **Exceptional Teamwork** – people with the right skills and attitudes working together.

4. **Commitment to Organizational Success** – individual and corporate ownership for achieving our common goals.

5. **Innovation and Renewal** – a willingness to try new approaches and encourage fresh ideas.

6. **Energizing, Encouraging Culture** – respectful, supportive and solution oriented.

7. **Pervasive Leadership** – people throughout the organization regardless of role actively working to develop each of the first six attributes.

Our journey never ended. We continued to face challenges but with the new approach and positive culture we worked together to address them and achieved excellent, sustainable results.

The summary of leadership roles and commitment that opened this book was the start of our rebuilding – of our renewed commitment to success. At that point there was need for hope, a light to give a sense of direction in a dark time. The thoughts expressed were not complete, having not yet endured the crucible of experience, but they opened the dialogue. That summary and the many discussions that followed provided an alternative to our underlying leadership weakness. Together, we expressed hope, built commitment and encouraged the leaders throughout the organization to join the battle.

No doubt, you too, are on this journey. You are seeking a better, more fulfilling life. You strive to achieve more, to bring value, to encourage others and, together, achieve goals that today seem out of reach.

Your title is not important. It is not a matter of position or authority. Leadership is not defined by the organizational chart whether you serve in a company, a non-profit organization or a social club. Leadership is about seeing what can be – the value that can be created – and enlisting others to join you in making it a reality. It is a journey worth taking.

Our purpose is to help in your journey – to stimulate your ideas and commitment. We encourage you to join us by developing the concept of pervasive leadership and applying it in your leadership role. It is a journey that will reward you and your organization deeply.

Application: A Leadership Crisis

1. Reflect on a time when your team (work, family, sports) was successful. Grade the importance of each of the "Seven Characteristics of Successful Organizations" listed above in that success. How was each attribute exhibited?

2. Consider a current personal or work challenge you face in terms of the same characteristics. Where are the strengths? What areas are adversely affecting performance?

3. Define how you can reinforce one characteristic that is strong and how you can strengthen just one that is not. Who do you need to work with to accomplish your plan?

"My son, if you receive my words, and treasure my commands within you, so that you incline your ear to wisdom and apply your heart to understanding; Yes, if you cry out for discernment and lift up your voice for understanding, if you seek her as silver and search for her as for hidden treasures, *then you will understand the fear of the Lord, and find the knowledge of God."*

Proverbs 2:1-5 NKJV

III
CLARITY OF PURPOSE

Energizing the organization by internalizing our reason for existing

"Every person, every organization has a purpose for being, that is not the question. Is it a worthy purpose, a passion that provides meaning and benefits society?

That is the question to be answered."

Every person has a purpose? Yes, we are unique – no one else has your personality, skills, experiences and passions. Each of those contributes to your value, your reason for existing. Indeed, the question is not whether we have a purpose, but whether it is meaningful and whether we are achieving it.

The same is true with organizations, whether it be a government department, a company, a university or church. We organize to accomplish something of value – a goal that cannot be accomplished by an individual. Again, the challenge is to define your organization's purpose in a way that inspires life, energy and commitment– to provide meaning in what we do.

You may have heard the ancient story of three stone masons working on the same project who were asked what they were doing.

- The first said, "Putting in my time, just hoping to get paid".
- The second responded, "Laying these stones perfectly, building a wall my sons will be proud of".
- "I'm building a cathedral to encourage the worship of the living God", exclaimed the third. "It will be a magnificent center of worship for generations to come!"

What are you doing? What is your organization achieving? How is it providing for the needs of its members and society as a whole? Why is this organization worthy of the effort that you and others are expending on it? These are the questions we need to answer, unless "putting in my time" or "just hoping to get paid" is all we expect.

The challenge is to define your organization's purpose in a way that inspires life, energy and commitment to achieving a worthy goal.

While most organizations have "purpose" or "mission" statements, often they are not effective. In many cases the words are too general to be compelling and do not appear to be related to our everyday tasks. As a result, mission statements often decorate the walls or annual reports, but have little relevance to everyday activities.

Examples of these limited value statements include:

"Becoming a world class performer"

"Healing people by providing stellar medical care"

"Being the best in our industry – the cable provider of choice"

"Rewarding share owners with outstanding returns"

Words, alone, do not define organizational purpose, but they are a start. An effective purpose statement is more than just a catchy phrase. It creates a picture of what we aspire to accomplish in terms of benefits, not just actions. It should reflect who we are and why our organization matters. An effective purpose statement should have the following attributes:

- Compelling - developing an emotional tie by expressing why our organization matters - the value it brings to society. It provides the reason that we give our best efforts to achieve the goals.

- Clear and concise – creating a picture of success for the team members and those they serve.

- Provide "line of sight" between the activities of individuals and subgroups in supporting the overall goal.

- Reflect the organization's core values and culture.

- Focus on achievement instead of philosophy.

While a written purpose statement is a start, it is when leaders throughout the organization routinely refer to it as a guiding principle and demonstrate it through their actions, that it becomes truly effective. It's not the words that are important – it is the integration of the purpose and values into the culture that makes the difference. Yet, too often, we overlook this essential element and, in doing so, miss an essential prerequisite for lasting success.

What is your organization's purpose?

"Creating a delightful pizza experience while drawing family and friends together"

"Providing an automobile that is a delight to drive while providing safe, reliable transportation"

"Providing hope for dysfunctional families by….."

"Assuring the safety and energy efficiency of buildings constructed in Springfield County"

"Sharing the joy of knowing Christ and the hope of eternal life"

Each of these is a start – a statement reflecting the purpose and value of the organization. In some cases, such as the pizza parlor, the simple statement may be adequate. Others, such as "Providing hope for dysfunctional families", will benefit from additional clarification by adding information about who, where and how.

The essential leadership element is defining a purpose that is meaningful to each member of the team – one that inspires them to excel. Like the stone mason, a pizza delivery woman will likely have a different approach to her job if she sees that she has a significant role in creating a delightful family experience instead of just delivering a meal, collecting the payment and hoping for a big tip.

We applied these concepts in clarifying the purpose of our electrical generation station. Working with a small group of leaders, we developed the following purpose statement: *"Advance society by providing safe, reliable and affordable electrical power."*

The written statement is simple. When discussed with employees and the public it becomes compelling by expressing the value of reliable power in terms of life-saving medical technology, reliable public transportation, advances in communication and the benefits of home heating and air conditioning. By doing this, we are defining an important role since a critical differentiator between an advanced society and third world poverty is the availability of reliable power.

The linkage between this important high level goal and the actual work done by employees could be emphasized in large and small group conversations. We consistently referred to our purpose during decisions concerning maintenance activities, equipment upgrades, personnel training, leadership development, etc. The hierarchy of goals; namely, safety then reliability and lastly cost were emphasized throughout the plant and integrated into the decision making process. The value of this clearly stated linkage was realized when craftsmen began taking initiative to fix important equipment instead of deferring degraded equipment to engineering to justify its acceptability. As a result, the repairs enhanced safety and reliability and, as a result, cost.

This example is just one of a multitude demonstrating pervasive leadership. We started by engaging leaders throughout the organization in refining the high level mission so that it had direct meaning to each team. Our intent was to establish a "line of sight" between each group's activities and the overall purpose of the organization. Individuals in all parts of the organization began making better decisions since they both understood the organizational goals and saw how they directly supported their achievement.

Another important aspect of a meaningful purpose is the ability to measure progress toward achieving the goal. In the power station purpose statement, it is easy to measure power production, in terms of gigawatt hours and reliability, in terms of unscheduled plant shutdowns. Each of these metrics was linked to individual organizations and the individuals. In other cases, customer surveys or stakeholder ratings may provide the needed insights.

Ultimately, it is leaders who define the broader organizational purpose creating a clear and compelling picture of whom we are and why our product or service is important. A high level, written purpose statement is a start. Leaders then personalize this purpose for each subgroup and individuals in those groups. Pervasive leadership is expressed when people throughout the organization refer to these goals in making hard decisions and holding other groups and managers accountable for those decisions. It is one step in creating a healthy, performance driven culture.

There is one other important concept we should consider in closing. What if you don't feel a compelling purpose? What if you don't have passion for your organization and the service it provides?

If you are a leader without a sense of purpose, it is time for a change. First, exercise your leadership skills to better define a truly meaningful purpose and gain support of others by applying the insights from this book. If that is not successful or you can no longer support your organization's purpose you need to change organizations!

Summary

Every organization has a purpose for existing, but this purpose may not be clear and compelling to either the team members or the people it serves. A written purpose statement is a beginning, but must become pervasive – providing guidance and energy to the organization. This purpose is the foundation around which all other aspects of organizational successes are built. It gives meaning to the team's unique and significant role.

Application: Clarity of Purpose

1. What is your team's purpose - not in terms of what you do, but in terms of what you aspire to accomplish – the value you provide? How does it enrich both the team members, the organization and society?

2. Work with your team to clarify and strengthen its sense of purpose. Ask questions and actively listen to their responses over the course of a few weeks before attempting to develop or revise the written purpose statement.

3. Consider how you can "live" this purpose and encourage others to do the same. How can you relate it to your actions and the team's decisions each day? How do the others respond to your initiative?

"Brothers, I do not consider that I have made it on my own. But one thing I do: forgetting what lies behind and straining forward to what lies ahead, I press on toward the goal for the prize of the upward call of God in Christ Jesus."

Philippians 3:13-14 ESV[ii]

IV
INTUITIVE, EFFECTIVE PROCESSES

Defining how we will achieve our goals

"Intuitive, effective processes ensure the quality of our product while respecting the individual – freeing us to accomplish those things that only people do well!"

Henry Ford is credited with bringing the assembly line concept into commercial prominence. It increased the speed of manufacturing and provided consistent quality at lower cost. While these early processes transformed manufacturing, they did not truly engage the intellect and judgment of the assembly line worker – those talents were reserved for those developing the process.

Have you ever faced a complex task and not really known where to start? If it's important, you either figure it out or ask for help. The power of defining a routine for our normal activities is to free us up to do those things that only people do well – developing wisdom from information, solving problems and developing positive relationships with others important to our success. The classic assembly line is better left to technology by using machines and computers to perform routine tasks.

Our purpose defines both **what** we intend to accomplish and **why** it is worthy of our efforts. Our process defines **how** we will accomplish these goals. We all have processes for accomplishing our tasks – they may be inconsistent, haphazard and inefficient, but everyone develops steps for completing any task from ordering lunch to launching a rocket into space.

Intuitive, effective processes are essential for organizational success. Without them we do not gain the full value of our efforts, we do not gain commitment from our team and we will not effectively support those who depend on our organization. Ineffective processes create frustration and waste, while effective approaches multiply effectiveness, create enthusiasm and encourage us to apply our heart and mind, in addition to our hands, to achieve the worthy goals.

Effective processes multiply our effectiveness by committing our hearts and minds to those areas that are essential for success.

The first question we need to address is whether our processes are effective - assuring consistency and quality. Secondly, are the processes efficient, maximizing the value of our talents? Achieving these goals is a fundamental role of leaders and a clear reason for expanding the definition of our "leadership team". When "pervasive leadership" is present, many people become "process owners" committing their best efforts for the organization.

Simply stated, a process is a series of steps taken to complete a task. It should have a logical sequence and will often be integrated with other activities that can be accomplished in parallel. For example, we are all generally familiar with the assembly line process for building a car. Assembling an engine is a separate process, consisting of many steps, that is merged with the basic structure of the car at the appropriate time on the assembly line. The same thoughts apply to other major components; body panels, interior components, wheels, etc. The goal is to bring all of the right parts together, effectively assembled and presented at the proper time to support the overall goal of providing a properly assembled, high quality vehicle.

Key goals in establishing an effective process include:

- Clearly state the purpose of the process. What is the product or service? What are the essential attributes and quality standards?

- The process should include a logical sequence of repeatable steps that make sense to the individuals implementing it.

- Critical steps, those that must be performed correctly to ensure quality, should be clearly identified.

- Simple checks to ensure that critical parameters are achieved should be identified and acceptance criteria clearly defined.

- Routine, repetitive steps should be automated to the extent possible, freeing people to anticipate and resolve unexpected issues and ensure quality.

- Responsibility for completing each step should be well defined with particular emphasis on the transition among work groups.

Too often our processes are cumbersome, providing many administrative steps that do not create value and discourage innovation. Steps that don't add value should be eliminated – particularly bureaucratic reviews or approvals.

How do we best establish or evaluate effective processes? The first principle is to involve those closest to the work – those who implement the process. It is also important to involve others who can ask the tough questions concerning the logic and value of steps. Subject matter experts, individuals from interfacing organizations, knowledgeable and inexperienced workers as well as managers should be involved.

As a starting point, gather a small group of employees to review one of your important but relatively simple processes. (Guidance on selecting the team is included in the "Teamwork" Chapter) The process review team should start by considering these questions:

- Does the process and its controls ensure that the product has acceptable quality? If not, what are the missing attributes?

- Is the process understandable by a knowledgeable, intelligent person who was not involved in its development? Where do they question the value added by steps or requirements?

- Is the process actually implemented as defined by procedures? If not, why? Do employees take shortcuts to eliminate unneeded effort or add steps to ensure quality?

- Where are the "choke points", those places that limit the speed in which the product is provided? Are the choke points required to ensure quality? In some cases these process restrictions result from limited resources or unneeded administrative burdens which can be resolved.

- Does the process have unneeded steps? Does each step add value? Do quality inspections and approvals truly add value?

As noted before, establishing effective, efficient processes is a key leadership function. There are at least five leadership roles in defining processes; namely,

- Defining the product and required attributes, such as, quality.

- Providing the organization and resources needed to implement the process.

- Overseeing the process and product to ensure that it is effectively implemented and achieving the desired quality.

- Encouraging innovation and process improvement and resolving barriers that inhibit process changes where needed.

- Interacting with other groups who interface with the process to ensure that the needed support and transitions are effective.

The first leadership role is directly tied to the organization's purpose. The broad purpose may include many sub-elements; design, procurement, manufacturing, marketing, sales, etc. Yet, each of these sub-processes can be defined as a series of steps.

Note that the first two roles are typically performed by people having traditional management positions and roles. The others can be performed by any employee. In fact, the most effective organizations are those where the people closest to the actual work have primary responsibility for monitoring and improving the process.

The questions and actions noted above can be used to evaluate existing processes. It is particularly important to consider the "choke points" and the interfaces where different organizations come together in the process.

> In effective organizations, the people closest to the actual work have the primary responsibility for monitoring and improving the processes.

Let's consider a simple example; A process for matching organizational volunteers to needed roles in a non-profit organization so that the needs of people being served are met. An example may be church ministry to meet the unique needs of single mothers in a low-income section of town. At a high level, this involves following, linked sub-processes:

Figure 1 Simple Process Flow Chart

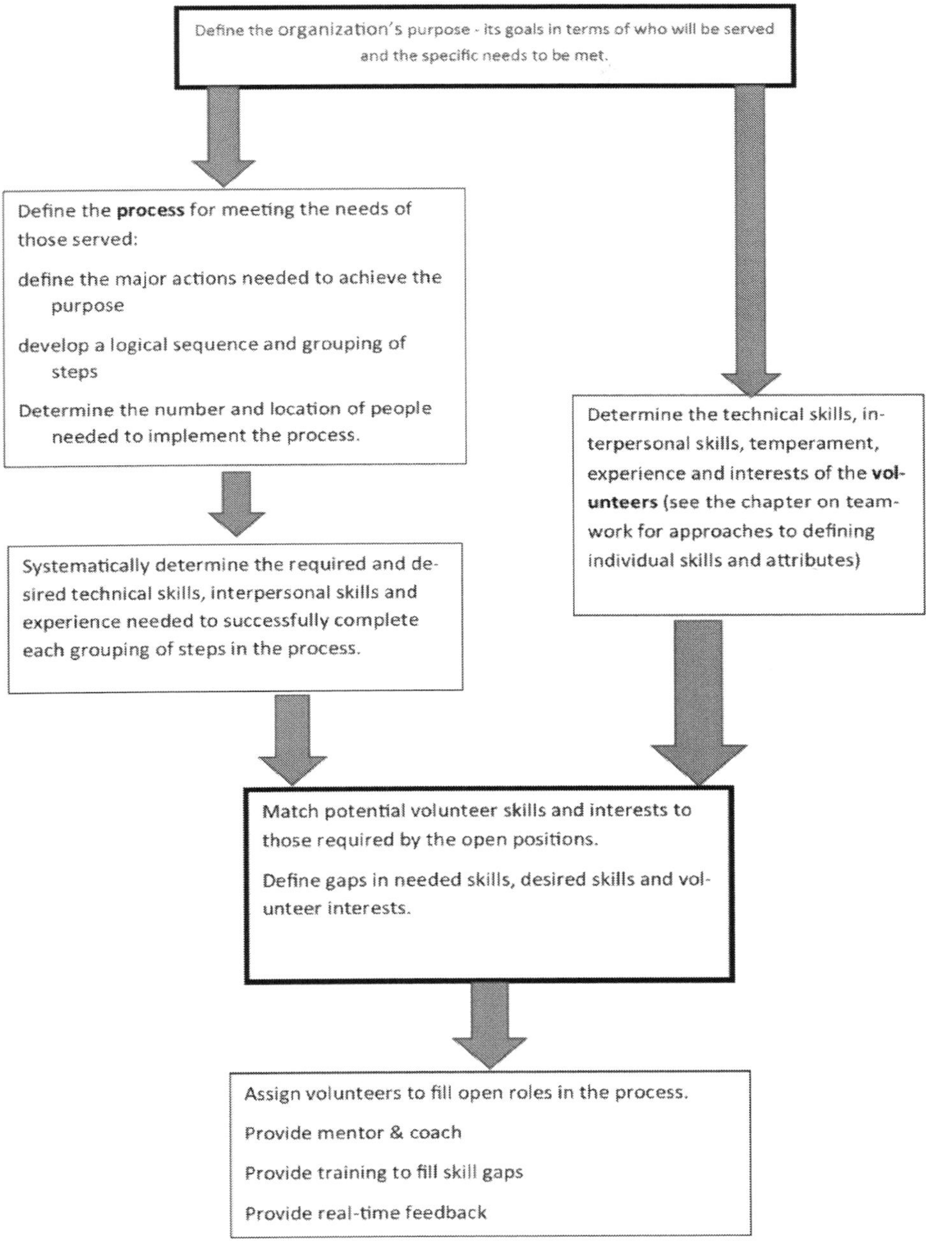

Define the organization's purpose - its goals in terms of who will be served and the specific needs to be met.

Define the **process** for meeting the needs of those served:

define the major actions needed to achieve the purpose

develop a logical sequence and grouping of steps

Determine the number and location of people needed to implement the process.

Systematically determine the required and desired technical skills, interpersonal skills and experience needed to successfully complete each grouping of steps in the process.

Determine the technical skills, interpersonal skills, temperament, experience and interests of the **volunteers** (see the chapter on teamwork for approaches to defining individual skills and attributes)

Match potential volunteer skills and interests to those required by the open positions.

Define gaps in needed skills, desired skills and volunteer interests.

Assign volunteers to fill open roles in the process.

Provide mentor & coach

Provide training to fill skill gaps

Provide real-time feedback

Summary

The goals of an organization can be met through a series of logical steps defined as processes. The processes can be organized into logical sub-processes and the required actions, knowledge, skills and attributes required for their completion.

Process development is dynamic, always seeking improvement. The pervasive leadership model engages both formal and informal leaders in process improvement with the goal of improving both efficiency and quality.

Application: Intuitive Effective Processes

1. Reflect on the concept of a process as a series of steps to logically and efficiently achieve a goal. Add your personal insights to develop a clear picture of an effective process.

2. Develop a simple diagram of the steps required to achieve a team goal. Clarify the critical steps - those that must be accomplished as planned to achieve the desired goal. Add sub-elements under each critical step.

3. Highlight the steps that currently impede achieving the goal. Typically these are interfaces among groups. Work with others to clarify how the process and interfaces should work and agree on actions to improve their effectiveness.

"Let all things be done decently and in order."

1 Corinthians 14:40. ESV

V
EXCEPTIONAL TEAMWORK

Qualified, motivated individuals working together to achieve a worthy, common goal

"We organize to accomplish more than we can as individuals, but it's only when we truly work together, with each individual contributing their unique and significant skills, that organizational magic flourishes.

If success was based on raw talent, the 2004 USA men's basketball team would have been awarded the Olympic gold medal without playing a game. The USA entry was often referred to as the "Dream Team". It included many of the of the NBA's upcoming stars; LeBron, Wade, Starbury, Duncan, and Iverson. In the end, it was more about teamwork than individual talent with the USA team suffering three losses including a 92-73 defeat by Puerto Rico, a commonwealth of only four million people. The team struggled to win the bronze metal and lost more games than USA Olympic teams suffered in all previous Olympiads combined. Team work often trumps talent both in sports and more traditional organizations.

If, as discussed in earlier chapters, we have defined our purpose and the processes we use to accomplish our goals, it is time to consider who will do the actual work. Who, in terms of individuals and teams, will implement the processes to provide our products and services? As noted in the last chapter, defining the process requires that we consider the people that will implement it. Either we need to build the process around the team members' existing skills or develop the team's skills to match those demanded by the process.

Leaders must invest their efforts in developing the team upon which success depends, not spending precious time writing policy and procedure manuals

Generally, both options should be melded, but in the end, the second approach is generally more viable. This requires a systematic approach - both in defining the required skill set and then selecting and developing the team members who will master these skills. Only then will our organization truly prosper. Yet this remains a major challenge since most organizations are not skilled in this essential role. Too often they spend more effort on developing policy manuals than they do on selecting and developing the teams upon which their success depends.

Consider the "job descriptions" in your organization. Is there a clear linkage between the specified job skills and those required to excel at the position and assure the organization's success? Typically, the job requirements are stated in terms of education and experience. For example, a typical position requirement is a B.S. degree in engineering with six years of progressive experience. Perhaps, there is a bit more detail, such as, six years' experience in either automotive design engineering or test engineering. The questions not answered by this approach include: true capability, ability to make decisions, resolve problems and bring out the best in others as a part of a team. In some cases, interpersonal skills and teamwork are considered during the hiring process, but typically this occurs when people first enter the organization and not when considering people for specific career assignments.

Individual and team success depend on a host of interrelated attributes. Knowledge, skills and experience provide a foundation for completing the required tasks and exhibiting sound judgment. But what about interpersonal skills, initiative, drive, judgment and attitude? Aren't these the important "team" skills? The players on the 2004 men's Olympic basketball team had greater ability than those they played against, yet they played as individuals and lost.

We won't discuss the theory of teamwork - that is generally well understood. Instead, we focus on three interrelated aspects of teamwork and the leadership roles in developing them. Two of the aspects are commitment and culture. These are covered in following chapters. The third is matching and developing team member skills to the process needs - the major item to be explored in this chapter.

One important role of a leader is to consider these broader attributes and then selecting and developing the team to truly meet the demands of the process. The leader's role is to meld them – to both improve the process and develop the team that will implement it.

In most cases, we are not starting from scratch with either the process or the team that will implement it. Success demands that we integrate the two; yet, this is rarely done in a systematic way. Assuming that the process is reasonably well defined, let's define the individual and team attributes that are essential for its effective implementation by considering the following areas:

> *The capability of the individuals must match those required by the process they are to implement. Too often, we only consider the technical skills while the temperament and attitude are just as important.*

- *Intellectual knowledge* – basic understanding of the technology or business. Often provided through education or formal training, for example in engineering, accounting, electronics or sales contracts.

- *Skills* - capability to perform physical and mental tasks, such as repair a computer or analyze data to determine tax liability. These skills often result from the application of education and training.

- *Experience* - ability to understand higher level reasoning, make sound judgments and solve complex problems.

- *Personality or temperament* - ability to demonstrate effective interpersonal skills and teamwork. Examples include the ability to translate ideas into meaningful actions, balancing alternatives, social awareness and clarity of communication. While many of these attributes are inherent, they can be developed as well.

- *Attitude and passion* - intrinsic desire to serve in the required roles resulting in commitment of discretionary effort to add value.

Let's develop a few of these in more detail:

Knowledge, skills and attitudes (KSA) can be defined and developed using a systematic approach such as that defined by Bloom's[1] taxonomy of learning. This process includes the systematic review of the tasks, processes and technology to determine the required KSA and then developing training to provide the needed competencies. A simple starting point is to gather a group of experienced, high performing team members with an educational technologist to develop a listing of the KSA. Key leadership roles include ensuring that these KSA are accurate and develop methods to assure that the incumbents possess them. People tend to be more committed and successful when their knowledge and skills match those required by the job.

---

[1] www.en.wikipedia.org/wiki/bloom's-taxonomy

Experience is developed by actively engaging team members in all phases of the process, including resolution of process and quality problems. It is expanded through temporary assignments to other interfacing groups. Learning is enhanced by aligning the individuals with highly experienced mentors and assuring a wide range of insights.

Personality or temperament are also important. There are many personality profiles that are useful for helping individuals and organizations develop stronger teams. The Myers Briggs Type Indicator[2] [3](MBTI) is one useful example. The MBTI describes our temperament in terms of preferences that affect our behavior patterns. For example, are we energized by people or by thoughts and ideas? Do we make decisions quickly or do we like to keep our options open. Are we energized or drained by being with a group of people. In this model, there are sixteen different preference groupings although, in reality, it is a continuum along four groups of differing preferences.

- Consider a team[4] role that requires a strong focus on reviewing objective data to verify that key product attributes are met and identify adverse trends using a "rules based" approach. Someone with an introspective, detailed, objective

---

[2] www.meyersbriggs.org

[3] Please Understand Me II, by David Keirsey, Prometheus Nemesis Book Company, 1998

[4] www.bestfittype.com

decision making temperament is a good match. In MBTI terminology, an ISTJ fits this role well.

- In a second example, consider a person who coordinates work among three different workgroups to resolve of emergent problems. There is a wide range of emergent problems with differing priority and a varying mix of skills needed for their resolution. As a result, the ability to optimize the assignment of resources from different work groups will be more important than in the prior example. The ability to see the bigger picture, assign priorities and develop flexible approaches is likely required - a MBTI ENTP may be well suited to this role.
- Now consider the implications for reversing these roles. The people oriented communicator who seeks options and possibilities will likely struggle with a detailed, objective data analysis job. Likewise the ISTJ will likely struggle with the lack of definition and ever-changing priorities of the workgroup coordinator role. Both roles are essential, but the best value comes from matching the natural temperament to the job demands.

These teamwork concepts should be expanded to other applications. For example, consider the mix of craft personnel in the maintenance group of a factory. While all may have excellent basic skills, some will likely focus on mechanical components while others focus on electrical systems or control systems. Even within these areas there will likely be sub-specialties. The question is whether we have the optimum distribution of skills to meet the work requirements. In addition, some may have temperaments more suited to trouble shooting which requires higher level diagnostic skills as compared to another person who is better suited to routine surveillances where the objective is to test and calibrate equipment to defined standards.

A second, more challenging example is that of first line supervisors. Supervisors are the bridge; defining the goals and expectations of managers for the people who must actually achieve them. Are these supervisors selected based on their ability to communicate and encourage commitment? Do they reinforce each other when applying performance expectations or rewarding high performance? Are they developed as a team and provided development opportunities to assure that they are capable of performing their supervisor role comfortably, gaining the respect of all those they serve?

Another important, yet often overlooked, aspect of teamwork is problem solving. How often have you seen management pull a team together to address a valid issue only to find the team to be ineffective? Application of High Impact Teams (HIT), cross-functional teams, etc. is valid, but only if properly implemented. Based on our experience, there are several important factors in gaining the value from such teams. These include:

- Clearly define the problem in terms of its scope and importance.

- Evaluate the cost of implementation, both in financial and human impact terms. Perform a robust review of potential "unintended consequences". It is important to include individuals on the team who provide these perspectives.

- Optimize the team composition. It is essential to include individuals closest to the problem with their wealth of practical experience, however, these individuals often have a limited paradigm that hinders their ability to see innovative solutions. There is value in including people with process knowledge but not directly responsible for the specific area being addressed. Examples include individuals from other organizations that interface with the process being evaluated, millennial generation team members who have strong social awareness and technical savvy as well as the classic subject matter experts. Typically five to ten members is optimum since this allows diversity of experience while allowing each member to fully participate.

- Ensure constructive interaction among team members. Social perceptiveness of team members – the ability to read the emotions and insights of others – should be among the key selection criteria for team members. It is this social awareness that forms the foundation of "collective intelligence". The value of using a group is only realized by encouraging active participation by all team members to develop solutions that may not otherwise be explored. Generally, this requires face-to-face meetings where emotions can be expressed and spontaneous discussion encouraged.

- Provide management support. Line leaders have three important roles; namely; assure that the problem is properly defined, help assure that the broader implications of proposed solutions are considered and actively support implementation of the recommendations. These roles are often overlooked. Successful implementation of recommendations often requires a "champion" with the leadership skills and authority to address the normal organizational reluctance to implement meaningful change.

Effective use of teams to improve the organization's effectiveness is a hallmark of leadership. Developing team members in this art is an important step in developing leaders and the concept of "pervasive leadership".

Summary

The leader's role is to understand the valid job requirements in terms of technical skills, attitudes and temperament and then select and develop individuals to fill these roles. Where leadership is pervasive, this responsibility is actively pursued throughout the organization. Individuals and teams throughout the organization will look at both the process and existing talent, seeking methods for improving performance.

This selection and development process can become a highly constructive, energizing experience as people sense that they truly fit in the organization and their contribution is valued. Work loses its negative connotation when people are using their skills and natural abilities in achieving a worthy goal.

Application: Exceptional Teamwork

1. What are the collective knowledge, skills and attitudes required to achieve your team's goals? Consider the education, experience and personality profiles that best meet these needs.

2. Consider your team. What are its most prominent strengths? What weaknesses challenge its performance? What opportunities exist to strengthen the team and its contribution? What threatens to make the team ineffective? How can you, individually and as a team, strengthen performance?

3. Understand your personality - your individual preferences, strengths and gaps - to gain an understanding of how you can best serve the team. Specifically gain insights concerning your social awareness and ability to draw out the best in others.

"For by the grace given to me I say to everyone among you not to think of himself more highly than he ought to think, but to think with sober judgment, each according to the measure of faith that God has assigned. For as in one body we have many members, and the members do not all have the same function, so we, though many, are one body in Christ, and individually members one of another. Having gifts that differ according to the grace given to us, let us use them..."

Romans 12:3-6 ESV

VI
COMMITMENT TO ORGANIZATIONAL SUCCESS

Individually placing the organization's success above our personal desires

"Commitment to a cause is a deeply held value, one that is intrinsic, not motivated by lectures or urging, but through deeply held beliefs.

It is this intrinsic power that unleashes the best we have to offer."

"We are preparing to shut the plant down since it is not clear we can repair the transformer in the allowed time," the site manager said.

I was four states away attending an industry conference and had earlier asked about the repair plans and status. There had been little clarity about contingency plans if the direct repair was unsuccessful. The transformer was a regulatory requirement since it provided power to critical systems, but there were options both for the repair and for alternate power supplies.

Now, as I was ready to board the plane for the return trip, it appeared that the options had been set aside. Shutting the plant down was now the "plan" since it was unknown how long it would take to obtain replacement parts.

Shutting down the plant was no minor decision. While we would not hesitate to do so if there was a safety concern, it was costly in terms of the impact on employees' personal lives and the direct loss of over two million dollars of revenue each day.

I called again when I arrived at my home airport, hoping for a more optimistic report. There was not one. Again, it was not clear that robust alternatives were being considered. I requested that the leadership team meet with me in an hour. The site manager was not enthusiastic about my request, so the expectation was clarified – the time, location and attendees specified.

Upon arriving at the plant, my first stop was at the transformer – the place where repairs were being made. But they weren't – no one was there. I went to the electrical shop, assuming that they were calibrating the electrical components which were the source of the problem. I found only two electricians – they were awaiting the work package and parts, but did not know when either would arrive. The story was similar when I talked with the work planners and warehouse crew – no one knew the actual status and there was no clear path to success.

When I arrived at the meeting room, only half of the key leaders were there. The others had gone home hours ago, before the extent of the problem was known. It was, after all, Friday. The status report I received from the managers was not accurate – not reflecting the information I had received from the people who were actually doing the work. In the end, we shut the plant down – I had only added frustration.

Ownership, commitment? Where were they? Where had I failed? How had a large organization, including well qualified leaders, accepted defeat so readily? Why had they not pursued multiple approaches to resolving the equipment problem? Why didn't they see the importance of fixing the issue before shutting the plant down?

Have you experienced a similar situation? Have you seen an urgent, important need for action that was not shared by your organization? Have you wondered why there was no sense of urgency in addressing needs and wondered how you can change the outcome?

Commitment comes from within. It is ownership of the result – it is being driven to achieve something that we personally value – not just giving a half-hearted effort. That ownership rarely comes from external urging. It is a result of individuals' emotional, intellectual and spiritual values being connected to the goal – the organization's purpose developed in the earlier chapter.

It is easy to assume that we have a common understanding of commitment. Yes, we generally know it when it is present, but what are the behaviors we see? How can we objectively evaluate our commitment or that of other members of our team? Here are some tangible indicators of strong commitment:

- Placing a high priority on organizational success even when conflicting with our personal comfort or risk aversion.

- Having an emotional response to the organization's performance, much like our response to our favorite sports team winning or losing an important game.

- Investing or personal time and energy into the quest for success, for example, thinking of how we can improve the group's performance while on vacation.

- Actively seeking new approaches to improving performance even when it is outside our experience or comfort zone.

- Discussing the organization and its success with friends and acquaintances.

- Supporting others to achieve organizational goals even if it detracts from our personal or group's accomplishments.

- Demonstrating high levels of personal behavior and integrity, believing that our example is how others view the organization.

So, the question becomes how do we develop these values in individuals so that it permeates the organization? Developing ownership and commitment is a leadership function. We start with internalizing the organization's purpose – explaining with intellectual and emotional rigor what we are to accomplish and why it is important. As expressed earlier, it is essential that this purpose is linked to individuals and their teams. Each of us must understand and feel the importance of our unique and significant role in accomplishing our goal. We must believe that what we are doing is important and of real value to the organization. We need a picture of success and our personal and team's essential role in completing that portrait and, with its accomplishment, a sense of personal victory.

The leader is the external agent – the one explaining, showing, and demonstrating the importance of the organization's achievement. It also requires us to express how the team and organization will be affected if we fail. Our role is to inspire that sense of personal and corporate pride. It is an integral part of the encouraging culture that we will discuss in the next chapter.

Commitment is gained only when we, as leaders, demonstrate ownership and personally request it from others in meaningful ways.

This is the essence of pervasive leadership. Success is only achieved when a "critical mass" of leaders in each team, each group and the organization as a whole understand the importance of what we are to achieve and are personally committed to achieving it.

It is expressed when individual team members step in to assure the team's success – even when it's not their direct responsibility.

It's when members of one team reach across organizational boundaries to improve the interfaces – to cover the gaps or weaknesses in the processes.

It is a leader's role to develop ownership in others by:

- Clarifying and emphasizing the individual's and the team's unique and essential role in achieving the organizational goal in clear compelling ways – touching the mind, heart and spirit.

- Demonstrating personal commitment to achieving the goals – visibly and overtly. The purpose is two-fold; to reinforce the importance of the organizational goal and to exhibit the actions, values and commitment required to achieve it.

- Asking the individuals and team how we can accomplish the goal. Ask about the barriers, the obstacles that are inhibiting their ability to achieve the goal. You will be amazed at their insights. Act on them – removing barriers that were identified is an essential step in building commitment.

- Personally asking for support – commitment from the team and team members. As a starting point, pick some important event or goal where you can make the request for commitment clear, specific and personal. Ask for support and some tangible expression of their support. Gaining a tangible expression of commitment is important – we are much more likely to meet our obligations if we have personally agreed to support them.

- Celebrate successes – recognize team accomplishments in ways that are meaningful to the group. We will discuss this more in the next chapter.

Yes, this is a tough order. It is not easy to truly follow these steps – your personal commitment is required. Yet, why do we expect others to be truly committed if we, as leaders, are not? We do not respond to "broadcast" requests for support, why should our team? Personal involvement, making the "need" real and relevant, is essential.

This process works. It was applied to address the "bad day" example discussed in Chapter II. The organizational goals were clearly stated – they were pictured in the form of a puzzle with each piece representing a key goal. When combined, the puzzle presented a beautiful picture of our plant – our success. We discussed these goals and their importance in small group meetings where the specific support needed from that group was debated. Barriers were identified and plans made for their resolution. Each employee was asked, personally, for their commitment and to signify it by placing their thumb print (yes – using an ink pad to put their thumbprint on the poster that was then placed in a prominent location) on the upcoming challenge – the "big event" that would determine our success for the year.

We were successful! In every respect we achieved and excelled. We won 43 to 0. And we did celebrate!

That was the start of a new path – one that led to success for several years. Developing commitment – intrinsic ownership – is hard, but absolutely worth the investment. It is a key step in building pervasive leadership and a constructive culture.

Summary

While true commitment comes from within, it is often inspired by other leaders who, through their personal passion, connect with the hearts and minds of others. Success is ensured when this passion is actively expressed throughout the organization - the essence of pervasive leadership.

Application: Commitment to Organizational Success

1. Rate your team's commitment to achieving the organization's goals using a 0 to 5 scale. Zero indicates a lack of commitment, three is marginally acceptable and five is a strong commitment. What are the indications of strong or weaker commitment?

2. Evaluate the contributors to areas of strong commitment in terms of the "Seven Characteristics of Successful Organizations" summarized in Chapter II. Do the same for areas lacking commitment.

3. Evaluate your personal commitment to the organization's success. Would a knowledgeable outsider rate your commitment as one, three or five? What objective evidence would they cite in making this assessment? Explore these conclusions in terms of the leadership principles discussed in prior chapters.

"Whatever you do, work heartily, as for the Lord and not for men, knowing that from the Lord you will receive the inheritance as your reward. You are serving the Lord Christ."

Colossians 3:23-24. ESV

VII
INNOVATION AND RENEWAL

Growing and adapting to meet the demands of our ever changing world

"Leaders welcome change, it's the old, the obsolete and ineffective that they fear, knowing that these are the very things that lead to demise!"

In today's world, success requires change! Innovation is essential in building our organization whether it is a university, business or non-profit organization. Many of today's economy cars outperform the beloved 60's "muscle cars" in braking, handling and fuel economy. Would you trade your smart phone for a rotary, land line phone that cost a quarter a minute for calls across the city? How about the hand calculator bought in the 1970's for the price of today's basic tablet computer? Just like obsolete products, organizations and processes must be renewed to incorporate advances in technology and society.

Clinging to the past may seem romantic, but very few organizations excel for more than a decade without innovation -

without renewing their products, processes, skills and technology. Even the most stable of organizations, the church, is seeing major changes as it addresses the spiritual needs of a dramatically changing society.

Change is the most difficult challenge most organizations face, yet few will thrive without renewing their products, technology and skills.

Yet, change is the most difficult condition for most organizations to master. We inherently seek stability. It provides a sense of security - we know the rules, we have developed competency and our role is valued. Often, both we and our organization have been successful with the current process and seem to forget the many changes that occurred over the years.

Take a moment to ponder that premise - what has changed in your organization? Look back a decade. Are you in the same position, working with the same people? Have you learned new skills? Are your products or services the same? Are you using the same computer and software? Is your interface with those you serve the same? Are the regulatory and administrative requirements the same? How about the customers you serve - have their expectations remained stagnant?

Change and innovation have occurred, that is not the debate. The real question is whether the change improved the product and process? A deeper question is whether you were involved in the change, helping define the desired outcomes, considering the potential "unintended consequences" and evaluating the benefits once the change was implemented?

In the pervasive leadership model, the answer to both of these questions is yes. Not every employee needs to be involved in every change. Change is not only initiated by those most directly affected. Yet, if you are directly affected by change in an organization with a pervasive leadership culture you will participate, making the change viable and achieving the overall goals.

One of the important roles of leaders is to look for opportunity to improve. The most fundamental change is to provide our current services better, faster and cheaper. The goal is to serve more people while reducing the cost and improving the quality. A second worthy goal of this type is to free individuals and organizations from monotonous tasks that do not require the intellectual, emotional and moral aspects of the human spirit.

There are generally two reasons for change; innovation and adaptation. For example, advances in technology often bring increased productivity and quality, but do not fundamentally change our purpose or processes. In other cases, demographic and social changes require adaptation to provide new products, services or approaches.

A second way of looking at change is by considering the extent and impact of the change. Changes are typically evolutionary, incremental steps in response to changes in technology or societal needs. In other cases, it can be transformational – dramatically changing our product or process. For example, consider the application of technology which as lead to fundamental changes in the way we share world events. Twitter®, Facebook® and YouTube® now provide instant access to world events where just a decade before we relied on traditional news reporters and camera crews.

How we classify changes is not important. The important mind set is to look for the need and opportunity to change. We do this by listening to those we serve and to our team. We analyze our processes and evaluate the value of our product. We seek the opportunity to broaden our service and apply innovative approaches that are transferred from other organizations or made possible by new technology. It is an ongoing process – one enhanced when pervasive leadership is present.

How do we identify the need and develop the plan for innovation or process improvement?

- When the need for change is driven by poor performance, it is good to look within. What worked in the past? What similar processes are working well in other parts of the organization?

- When the purpose of the change is to improve effectiveness and efficiency it is often best to assemble a team to review the process. Begin by looking at the delays, those places that tend to inhibit the flow of work or require excessive intervention. Listen to the leaders closest to the work - where are their challenges, frustrations and bottlenecks? They will often have the solution.

- When process or quality challenges have been clearly defined, it is beneficial to seek insights from our peers in other organizations. Typically they have faced similar challenges and developed solutions that we can adopt and enhance.

- If the need for change is driven by changes in technology, there may be a need for assistance from outside the organization to consider the challenges and implications.

- Another approach is to seek insights from unrelated industries. For example, many insights concerning flight crew dynamics developed by the airline industry were applied to operational crews at nuclear power plants.

The key in all cases is to challenge our paradigm. This generally requires that we look outside our work group and organization. Again, the role of the leader is first to identify the need for improvement - to recognize that frustration, delays and poor quality are generally a cry for innovation, not a sign of laziness or apathy. Where there is pervasive leadership, the recognition of and creative solutions for resolving these challenges come from within the organization.

To excel, leaders must be systematic in their approach to change. They must address the following aspects of any significant change:

- Benefit - clear definition of the purpose and value of the change.

- Magnitude - involvement of those closest to the change to define its breadth and depth.

- Cost - direct and indirect impacts on others. Unintended consequences must be considered and addressed.

- Risks – determine what can go wrong and the consequences of failure. Compensatory measures should be established to minimize both the probability and consequences of these failures.

- Implementation plan - full consideration of each of the above considerations

Leaders must accept some risk of failure; not all "improvements" work. While not desirable, failure is acceptable if it is not too costly and leads to deeper understanding that will be applied in the future.

How do we avoid costly failure? There are several methods that work well in the pervasive leadership model. The most important is to involve “thought leaders” from throughout the organization – those individuals who are known for questioning decisions and considering options. Listen carefully as they explore what needs to change and who will be affected, both directly and indirectly. Specifically review potential unintended consequences of the change and define the worst possible outcome. Then establish monitoring and controls so that compensatory actions can be taken to identify and correct adverse conditions before they become significant.

Here is a challenging example - approaches to staff reduction at two very similar, large businesses. In both cases, the application of technology, improved work processes and gains in employees’ skills and motivation resulted in more people than were needed to accomplish the company goals. In each case, the employees filling the unneeded positions were treated with respect and provided with similar good severance benefits. That is where the similarly ended.

- In the first case, targeted reductions were established by senior management. The decision was made to only seek volunteers willing to leave the organization in return for the severance benefits. This sounds like a great approach - right? It was not. The unintended consequences were profound. Most who left were high performing employees, newly hired engineers and well qualified technicians who had no problem in finding similar positions and enjoyed the "free money" as they pursued their new career. Fortunately many great employees remained – those who had built their career with us and were intensely loyal to our organization. Less fortunate was that many low performance employees remained - those with limited job skills and initiative. Another weakness of this approach was that it did not consider the workload within each group or the potential loss of critical experience. Collectively, this approach to staff reduction increased the workload and frustration of the many good employees who remained.

- In the second company, the separation process was selective with a combination of volunteers and targeted resignations. The need for change and selection process were clearly defined. Reduction targets were established by considering the work process, not solely by budgets. Leaders throughout the organization were involved in selecting the individual's leaving the organization and to assure that the right people and skills were retained. They actively involved the employees selected for retention in revising their processes to reflect the leaner organization which emphasized the importance of the new team in the organization's future. Both performance and morale improved.

A key reason for the success in the second example was providing a clear focus on the organization's purpose and the application of "pervasive leadership" principles. By involving people throughout the organization in the need for these changes, the benefits of improving processes and teamwork were realized. In addition, the impact of the changes were considered and steps taken to assure that they were constructive.

In most cases, changes are evolutionary and can be managed to gain their value. Sometimes, however, transformational change is needed. The challenge of major changes associated with true renewal or fundamental change in our products, processes or services is far greater than simple process improvements. These are changes to our fundamental business, products or approach. For example, electrical utilities desired to move into land development, communications, and emerging markets in the late 1990's. Nearly all failed.

Likewise, renewal is not easy. It is often hard to see the need for change or welcome the unsettling feeling it brings. Often there is frustration and inefficiency associated with change leading us to question whether the change is worth the cost, particularly when it is not well developed and impact on other organizational aspects is not considered.

How do we minimize the risk of transformational change? We start with clarifying the scope of the change and its anticipated benefits. Only then can we begin a systematic review by answering fundamental questions, such as:

- Do we have the experience and expertise to ensure success?
- Does it add to or build on our current core competence?
- Do we truly understand the new product or service?
- What is our core competency that the change builds on?
- Why are we better equipped to undertake this change than other organizations with similar interests and capability? What makes us the best organization to pursue this opportunity?
- Does it require renewal of skills and approaches for both the team and the individual?
- Does it change our basic mission or purpose, risking loss of focus?
- Does it increase our risk in a way that may adversely affect our core business? For example, what are the costs in terms of finances, reputation, etc?
- Does it distract key leaders and resources from our current, successful endeavors?

Leaders determine whether the change is worth the cost, and ensure it is well developed and that impact on other parts of the organization are considered. Leaders question change, not to block it, but to make certain that it is well planned and adds value.

Summary

In the end, change is inevitable. The leader's role is to ensure that the change is truly an improvement - that it adds value. Constant change leads to frustration and loss of focus. We need consistency and cannot excel on a "flavor of the month" approach to leadership. It is only through the pervasive leadership model that we welcome innovation and the true value it brings.

Application: Innovation and Renewal

1. Consider the process weakness you evaluated in Chapter IV. Reach out to an innovative team member to gain insights into how technology can improve the process.

2. Conduct an exercise with a broad based group of team members to consider how your product or process can be transformed to meet the challenges of the 21st century.

3. Take action to broaden your perspective or skills. For example, complete an assessment of your leadership style and effectiveness using one of the profiles referenced in the following chapter.

"Do not be conformed to this world, but be transformed by the renewal of your mind, that by testing you may discern what is the will of God, what is good and acceptable and perfect."

Romans 12:2 ESV

VIII
ENGAGING, ENCOURAGING CULTURE

Gaining the value of combined intelligence by lighting the fire of passion

"Developing a constructive culture, one in which all team members are respected and the organizational values are embraced, is a leadership imperative.

It cannot be delegated or ignored!"

A star professional football player made headlines by striking his future wife – knocking her unconscious – in a public place. The reason that this violence was remarkable had less to do with the rarity of such abuse, but that it was captured on a security camera. The media played and replayed the video while delving into other examples of domestic violence within the professional football community. While the pundits questioned whether football encouraged a culture of violence, the National Football League was slow to respond. Their public statements and sanctions lacked both clarity and conviction, implying that the events were isolated and not directly relevant to the culture of the sport. Only in following weeks did the league begin to take a strong stand and acknowledge its initial lack of leadership in establishing a positive culture.

All organizations have a culture – the collective set of values and beliefs that provide the framework for how we treat each other and what we accomplish. Too often, however, there is little focus on that culture – on evaluating whether it is actively supporting our purpose or impeding it. It is even less common that deliberate steps are taken to change the culture.

"Change values?" your may ask. "How can you challenge people's personal beliefs in this age of political correctness?"

Excellent question. Yet, there is an answer. We address culture by addressing its "artifacts", the behaviors. In that way we don't need to delve into philosophical discussions of values or motivations. There is no need to debate the validity of beliefs or what happened in the past. Instead, we discuss, model and encourage behaviors that meet the agreed to norms. Our first step is to help the organization define the desired culture in terms of engagement and behaviors. The questions is, "How do we expect to interact and how can we encourage each individual to embrace these behaviors?"

Let's start with those that we have already discussed; namely, our purpose, processes, teamwork and commitment. We all seek to accomplish something of value and to do it efficiently as a team. Those are attributes of a healthy culture – one that nearly all team members will embrace. We have explored the roles of leaders in developing these key concepts and the importance in involving a broad spectrum of the team in that process. In these actions, we have started to develop our desired culture.

As a next step, it is helpful to consider two aspects of culture:

First is the degree to which individuals are committed to and engaged in the organization's purpose. The second is how we interact with one another in terms of observable behaviors.

There are many ways to measure the engagement of team members. One of the most researched and accepted methods is the Gallup® Consulting Employee Engagement survey[5]. This survey determines the distribution of individuals that are engaged, not engaged and actively disengaged. According to Gallup, top performing organizations typically have about two thirds of the employees engaged and less than ten percent actively disengaged.

We build on the Gallup® approach by adding the pervasive leadership model. In our model we consider the following reference points on the commitment continuum:

- Pervasive leaders – those that are fully engaged and seeking to influence others. These are the "interveners" who actively seek to establish expectations, reach out to others, anticipate needs and solve problems. These are the team members who see their role as more than implementers, but as owners who

---

[5] Gallup Consulting® Employee Engagement – www.gallup.com/file/strategicconsulting/121535/employee_engagement

seek to improve the process and increase the engagement of others.

- Engaged implementers – those that are focused on outcomes and personally committed to achieving the organizational goals. These are the "active implementers" who are eager to support the organizational goals.

- Non-engaged implementers – those who work to externally defined expectations, but feel little personal connection to the outcome. These are the "passive implementers" who prefer comfort to accomplishment or are fearful of failure.

- Inhibitors – those who are actively disengaged, finding barriers to achieving their assigned roles and often drawing energy and focus away from the core work.

The goal in this model, like that of Gallup®, is to move people up the commitment continuum. Not all people will pick up the leadership mantel, but dramatic improvement occurs when 20-25% do. They form the catalyst to move others from the "non-engaged" to "engaged" category gaining the energy, insights and ability of the majority and making it less comfortable to be an "inhibitor".

We do not link these roles to positions in the organizational structure. You can have people with senior leadership titles who are disengaged. While the expectation is organizational managers are truly leaders, the power of pervasive leadership is that it permeates the organization – making the organizational chart more about function than influence on others. For example, a manager is responsible for budgets, reporting, etc. but may not be effective at inspiring others.

One specific responsibility that organizational leaders cannot delegate is addressing the "inhibitors". There are many constructive ways of achieving this; clarifying roles and expectations or finding another position that better matches their skills and interests, to name a couple. The important point is that inhibitors are not allowed to continue in that role – this is a major challenge in developing pervasive leadership.

The second aspect of culture is the organization's behavioral norms. These are the accepted ways that we interact with others and approach our assignments. We have discussed clarity of purpose, the value of processes, strong teamwork, commitment and innovation. In growing organizations, these are underlying values that our behaviors directly support. Yet, there are sub-elements to each and common behaviors that support all. Our goal is to identify and reinforce those that are most important.

In most cases, the organizational culture is neutral or positive but not well defined. In these cases, a fairly low-key approach often works to bring more focus and support on building positive relationships among individuals and groups.

The most basic elements of a positive culture are respect and trust. We show respect by the way we interact with each other. Speaking to each other respectfully and actively listening to understand others viewpoints are essential. Openness and actively involving others in decisions are key elements in building trust. Our actions must be consistent with our words and professed values.

When leaders throughout the organization apply these basic principles and support others in their application, positive change will flourish.

We experienced a straight forward example of this approach when there was a lack of respect and trust between "management" and the "bargaining unit" in a large organization. We started by jointly establishing simple ground rules: actively listening, using questions instead of judgmental statements, seeking common understanding, eliminating cursing and openly discussing the basis for decisions. We established a "word picture" of our desired behavior and held each other accountable for acting consistent with the desired behaviors. Most important was following through on promises. While it was not immediate, this simple approach was a major step in building respect and trust in the organization. With this foundation, morale, commitment and performance all improved.

After seeing success in our limited approach, we decided to take a more systematic approach to developing a positive culture. This simple approach was:

- Developing a broad list of observable behaviors that may be associated with constructive cultures. Where possible, several words with similar meanings were used to provide a broader, more understandable picture of the desired behaviors. A broad sampling of organizational members should be involved in developing validating the list. As a starting point, examples are provided in Table 1.

Table 1: Examples of Behavior Based Organizational Traits

Constructive Culture – Behaviors

Key Behavior	Similar Behaviors
Respectful	*Valuing, Listening*
Encouraging	*Supportive, Welcoming, Accepting*
Collaborative	*Involved, Engaged*
Innovative	*Creative, Adaptable*
Successful	*Achieving, Productive*
Authentic	*Sincere, Clear*
Systematic	*Organized, Planned*
Questioning	*Evaluating, Probing*
Caring	*Friendly, Compassionate*
Empowered	*Authorized, Responsible*
Aligned	*United, Consistent*
Energizing	*Inspiring, Compelling*
Honest	*Trustworthy, Truthful*

- Developing and implementing a simple survey using the selected words. The survey asks two questions concerning each word:

    a. How important is this behavior in achieving our goals?

b. To what extent do we currently demonstrate this behavior?

In addition, it was useful to allow "write-in" statements or words team members felt expressed important behaviors in support of the desired culture. It is important to get a strong majority of the organization to participate in the survey and to capture the results at a team level while assuring that the results are not linked to individuals.

- Analyzing the survey results to identify those few, core behaviors that are considered essential to a healthy work environment and those where there is the biggest gap between the desired and current demonstration of those behaviors. Once developed, these data should be summarized in a way that provides a clear, compelling picture of the desired culture and behaviors.

- Integrating the cultural picture into all aspects of the organization. Integration is essential and is a key role for leaders throughout the organization. Behaviors should be explored when reviewing both successes and challenges.

- In some cases, specific actions may be taken to encourage the desired behaviors where significant gaps are identified; however, the use of "campaigns" should be minimized. Developing the desired behaviors and drawing them into the culture is a process not an event. It's through integration, building them into our daily routine and discussions that they become real.

People throughout the organization should be involved in all phases of the process. This is a key role for the leaders – emphasizing the importance of pervasive leadership. This is clearly a time when there should be no surprises, no implication that the desired behaviors are developed by a secret group in a dark, smoke filled room.

A first step in the process (once again we rely on the "process" concept) outlined above is to define the desired organizational traits – those observable characteristics that define who we aspire to be and how we relate to one another. It is important that these be developed by the organization so that they become reality. Table 1 provides a potential starting point to help develop the concept. Once the few important characteristics are identified, they need to be defined in a compelling behavioral context. Examples may include:

- We are collaborative - involving the team in key decisions, valuing their contributions in strengthening our performance.

- We focus on success – both in the accomplishment and the process used to accomplish it.

Again, it is important to emphasize that the goal is not to develop high sounding phrases to hang on the

> *By developing a positive, encouraging culture we create an environment where leaders emerge, energy abounds and success flourishes.*

walls in an attempt to broadcast our values. Our purpose is to define who we are in terms of our relationships and behaviors. It is to establish expectations and integrate them into our daily conversations and, more important, our actions.

One imperative is that leaders, both formal and informal, hold themselves accountable to these behavioral standards. It's only when leaders openly discuss their personal shortfalls and welcome direct feedback that the culture will change.

There are also a few values and behaviors that we must discourage – those that must be overtly addressed through leadership and constructive peer pressure. The most prominent of these includes self-serving demands, arrogance and anger. In each case, individuals or groups expressing these behaviors are placing their personal interests above those of the broader team. Additional examples of unacceptable behaviors are dishonesty, cynicism and apathy. Again, it is through gaining support for the positive, constructive behaviors that the pervasive leadership approach can help identify and address these unwelcome behaviors before they adversely affect the organization.

While establishing a positive, performance oriented culture is important, it is not easy. In cases where there is not a healthy culture, a more rigorous process may be required.

In one company there was a deep rift between management and the skilled workers who were essential to its success following a union contract dispute. The interface between work groups was also stressed due to differing views on how the contract dispute was resolved. In this case, we decided that professional help was needed to rebuild trust and build a foundation to create a constructive culture. This process worked well, but required extensive leadership involvement and support from an external consulting company.

A company that has a comprehensive approach for building a constructive culture is Human Synergistics International[6]. They include a complete suite of products built around twelve behaviors. Their statistically validated process included methods for defining the existing organizational culture and related leadership behaviors. Their approach, coupled with strong leadership allowed us to address the underlying cultural challenges that stifled our success.

Summary

The success of any organization relies on a positive, success oriented culture. There are many approaches that may be applied, but the one mistake that many organizations make is not addressing the underlying culture. As noted in the opening of this chapter, there are times that the organization's culture stresses its very fabric. Leaders recognize these challenges and use them to make a transformational change in culture. Senior leaders must set high expectations. The value of the pervasive leadership approach is in clarifying the desired behaviors and encouraging people throughout the organization to reinforce them.

---

[6] Human Synergistics International® – www.humansyn.com

1. Research different methods for defining a positive, encouraging culture such as those discussed in this chapter. Use this information to refine the list of desired team behaviors summarized above.

2. Conduct a simple survey with team members and members of interfacing teams to define the desired behavior based culture. Work with the team to define how the desired culture with specific emphasis on how shortfalls in behaviors will be addressed.

3. Develop a constructive relationship with an individual who will provide valid, candid feedback to you both when your personal behaviors meet the desired standards and when they are not consistent with the expectations.

"But the fruit of the Spirit is love, joy, peace, patience, kindness, goodness, faithfulness, gentleness, self-control; against such things there is no law."

Galatians 5:22-23. ESV

IX
PERVASIVE LEADERSHIP

Expanding the circle of success by multiplying true leaders

"True leadership is not inherited, it is not an entitlement nor is it bestowed due to position. It is earned through an active commitment to the purpose, values and people of the organization. It is demonstrated by the courage to advocate and do the right thing, even when not expedient."

Pervasive leadership! This concept is expressed by leadership being distributed throughout the organization, not based on a hierarchy as in the classic military model. We have provided examples of it as we developed the importance of defining the organization's purpose, teamwork, commitment, innovation and culture. What is there to add? Let's start by comparing the implications of individual and pervasive leadership.

Purpose: While the overall purpose of an organization may be defined by a board of directors or executives, it is only empowering when the purpose is personal to work groups and individuals throughout the organization. It's only when they understand both the broader purpose and the unique role they play in achieving those goals that the publicized purpose takes life. When leaders at all levels link individual and team contributions to achieving a worthwhile goal, we give our best effort.

Process: While many organizations hire "experts" to design a process or continue to use those developed a decade ago based on then current technology, they will never achieve their full potential. It's only when individuals throughout the organization, particularly those "closest to the work", take ownership of the process that it has any real hope of being intuitive, effective and efficient. Again, this requires leaders, whatever their official title, to assess the existing processes, identify the weak links and enact changes to improve the quality and cost of the product or service. "Not my job," some may say. This means that pervasive leadership has not rooted in the culture.

Teamwork: Processes only work when the skills of the individuals match those required for success. With traditional, top down leadership, there is little focus on this critical aspect. When pervasive leadership exists there is a nearly magical ability to match those skills through a combination of process changes, developing the skills within the work group and realigning individuals' roles to match their strengths to the work flow.

Commitment: When leadership is distributed throughout the organization, ownership for accomplishing the organization's goals will be found. One of the key attributes of leadership is the sense of commitment and a passion for success. Pervasive leadership takes a stand when things are not going well, seeking to correct and address the underlying issues instead of waiting for "management" to respond.

Innovation: Traditional leadership is slow to change, innovate or adapt since it requires layers of justification and approvals. Pervasive leadership encourages those closest to the work to seek better methods, faster technology and stronger interfaces. Where individuals and groups have the authority to make changes, improvement flourishes. Of course, ground rules must be established, but with the philosophy of reaching across traditional organizational boundaries to achieve better results, change tends to be better thought out, more widely accepted and more beneficial.

Culture: The culture is a summation of the accepted behavioral norms of the organization. Establishing a constructive culture is a key leadership responsibility, perhaps only second to defining the organization's purpose. With pervasive leadership, the clarification and reinforcement of these behavioral norms is ever-present. There is less opportunity for a negative sub-culture to take root or an "us versus them" mentality to exist. Pervasive leadership is always encouraging, always intervening, always focusing on building a constructive team motivated by achievement.

Leadership: We return to the fundamental question. If pervasive leadership is so great, why isn't it pervasive in today's organizations? The answer is fairly simple – to encourage pervasive leadership requires

If pervasive leadership is so great, why isn't it pervasive in modern organizations?

that the hierarchical leaders give up some control – to accept that the people within the organization understand the goals and values of the organization and will faithfully work within that framework. It requires them to change their paradigm, moving out of their comfort zone. This requires either a brave manager or agreement within the traditional management structure to whole heartedly accept the new model. Both are rare.

So, with that in mind, how do we start? We start small, identifying a few applications for developing individual leadership skills by granting both the freedom and authority to make improvements. Likely candidates include process improvements, evaluation of new technology, developing a stronger personnel safety infrastructure or establishing key performance measures. No, planning the annual Christmas party or Independence Day celebration does not count!

Once the application is identified, preferably with active involvement of the work groups, the purpose, goals, budgets, constraints and feedback process should be clarified. The overall purpose of broadening individual involvement and leadership should be clearly established. The supporting, traditional leader must then move into the coaching role with a primary focus on supporting the team by providing the resources needed for them to be successful. The key attributes, purpose, process, teamwork, commitment, culture, innovation and leadership should be integrated into the plan. They must be discussed and modeled as a key element of the transition to pervasive leadership. The group must be set free to seek their purpose, apply their leadership and address their challenges.

The end goal is to empower all employees through a deep understanding and acceptance of their roles and responsibilities. It's about commitment to establishing a culture of success, of individual courage and passion for achievement. It's demonstrated when individuals at all levels seek to do the right thing instead of the previously accepted approach which resulted in mediocrity in both performance and spirit.

Pervasive leadership provides great value, yet there is risk. If all are accountable for results, is any one truly accountable? There will always be a role for the traditional, hierarchical leader. Organizations define certain responsibilities to individuals in certain positions. This is necessary and desirable – it provides order, it streamlines decisions, and it provides clarity and security. What are these unique roles of the traditional, hierarchical leader that relies on positional authority? Examples include:

- Providing clarity of purpose and priorities by helping the team see what is important now in terms of the longer-term goals.
- Defining organizational imperatives and constraints, such as, regulatory compliance, financial controls, budgets, staffing levels, etc.
- Establishing the framework for a constructive culture through actions and, when necessary, words.
- Developing leadership skills in others - giving them opportunity and accepting failures as a normal part of the learning process.

- Clarifying the organization's values, directly linking it to roles and responsibilities.

- Providing needed resources and breaking down barriers that impede organizational effectiveness.

- Disciplining team members in those few cases where they refuse to meet performance or conduct standards.

- Accepting responsibility for group failures, for understanding the underlying causes and implementing corrective actions.

- Assertively addressing events or issues that are not consistent with the organizations goals or culture.

- Communicating in times of crises – being the focal point for internal and external stakeholders.

As we close this chapter it is important to accept that not all people want to be leaders – many people are happier to work hard within defined roles. That is fine, there is a need for people who do real work to high standards. We should welcome them, but encourage them to support their peers who do want to lead. What we cannot accept are those who "lead" against us either actively or passively.

This book started with a passionate description of "what leaders do". It provided a general vision. The rest of the book has explained how an organization's power comes from within – from pervasive leadership. That is our quest, it is where we will find success and fulfillment.

Let's close with one additional example. During one of the organizational crises discussed earlier in the book, two bargaining unit employees suggested that we pursue gaining "STAR" status under the U.S. Occupational Safety and Health Administration's Voluntary Protection Program (VPP). This OSHA program is unique in recognizing three aspects of safety; high industrial safety performance, robust safety programs and a strong commitment to safety expressed throughout the organization. If all three are present, OSHA recognizes the organization with its highest level STAR recognition.

At the time, we were immersed in change with many improvement plans and priorities. The organization and leadership was stressed by the magnitude of the changes and our industrial safety performance was acceptable – actually one of our better areas. We were inclined to turn down the employees' offer citing the existing priorities and workload. The employees sensed our lack of enthusiasm but instead of accepting it, continued to explain the benefits which included an opportunity for management and bargaining unit employees to work together to achieve a goal we all supported.

I asked what they needed of me and the senior leadership team.

"Only your verbal support giving us the time to meet the program administrative requirements," they responded. "We will do the work."

How could I refuse? Yet, it was hard for me to get out of their way and let them achieve this important goal. I agreed and they accomplished the goal. We became one of the first organizations in our industry to achieve OSHA's STAR status. It was a bit humbling to admit that I nearly killed this important step in the organization's development but, in the end, it was an important step in my understanding of pervasive leadership – one of many!

Summary

Success requires that individuals throughout the organization accept ownership for achieving its goals. This is the essence of pervasive leadership and is developed through a systematic application of the seven principals of effective organizations. True leaders embrace these concepts and engage others in their application.

Application: Pervasive Leadership

1. Develop a list of leadership roles in your organization. Which ones are traditional, hierarchical roles and which can be distributed? Ask others on your team and interfacing teams to challenge the list - it is often hard to shift our traditional view of leadership roles.

2. Conduct a simple two to four hour workshop on pervasive leadership concepts and the list developed in application 1 above. Seek agreement within the team on applications of this concept in strengthening team performance.

3. Develop a personal list of areas where you can release some control to strengthen team commitment and develop leadership skills in other team members. Implement the plan.

"Where there is no guidance (leadership) the people fall (fail); but in a multitude of counselors (leaders) there is safety (success)."

Proverbs 11:14 NKJV (modified)

X

CLOSING – OR IS IT THE BEGINNING?

The quest for success never ends – it is an ever continuing journey

"Our quest is not about recognition, promotions or compensation. Our journey is about making a difference – about creating the future, enjoying life and knowing that our organization and society are better because we were committed to success."

As we bring this short essay to a close, we must ask "what next?" Do we file this, along with the other reference books that have preceded it? Or do we choose to apply its insights – to accept a new paradigm that defines leadership in terms of roles instead of titles? **Will we be the change** that is so clearly needed?

We have not focused on organizational charts or hierarchy. We have not discussed "fairness" or "opportunity". We have focused on pervasive leadership as the key to success. Opportunity abounds –

it's our role as leaders to seize it. In the pervasive leadership model there is plenty of opportunity for each of us if we define success in terms of:

- Creating a better product, process, or service to benefit society.

- Finding "our place" on the team – that place where we use our unique skills and personality to achieve a worthy goal.

- Seeing that a setback is not a failure, it is an opportunity to learn and grow.

- Growing personally by developing understanding, wisdom and compassion.

- Encouraging others to see the fullness of their potential and to reach for it.

- Building our legacy, our brand, day by day.

- Standing firm when encouraged to compromise our integrity or core values.

- Providing strength and stability in times of crisis.

- Sleeping well at night, in peace, knowing that what we accomplished is of value and that we did it with integrity.

These are the true measures of success. These are the things of lasting value, the things that we pass down to the next generation whether it be our organization or our children.

What will you do today? Will you take the first steps toward building a pervasive leadership team? Will you choose to become the leader that you, and others, desire to follow?

Developing pervasive leadership is not easy. It requires that we have the courage to release control – that we ask questions instead of directing others to meet our desires.

The first step in this quest is to develop our own leadership skills. The second is to encourage, model and develop pervasive leadership throughout the organization. Our goal in both cases is to create an effective team – an environment where we focus our talents and efforts on achieving a common purpose.

We begin by developing our own leadership skills, by becoming the leader that we want to replicate throughout the organization. We do this by understanding our own strengths and weaknesses by actively seeking input from others as we seek to help them.

What about tangible steps? Reading and applying the principles of this book is a great first step – you are already farther along than the majority of people who perused the cover. Here are some more thoughts:

- Understand yourself by using any number of personality profiles – Myers Briggs Type Indicator,

Birkman, and Organizational Cultural Inventory. There are many available at no cost through a simple web search.

- Understand and help shape the cultural leadership norms of the organization. Where does your style match that expected by the organization and where are there gaps? Where is there a need to change the norm?

- Gather a group of your peers to look at one aspect of a key process to identify the specific areas where it can be improved to achieve the desired outcome faster, cheaper and with better quality.

- Identify a peer who you respect and ask them to observe you and provide candid feedback both in areas where you excel and those where you can improve. Always thank them for the feedback, even when it hurts or seems unfounded – it is a gift.

Developing a pervasive leadership team involves two major components; the ability to ask insightful, provocative questions and the courage to take a stand in building a constructive culture.

What is the purpose of asking provocative questions, particularly when we know the answer? Why not just share our wisdom or, if it appears to be more constructive, we can just formulate our statement as a question? Our purpose is to gain support, to build a deep, intrinsic understanding for our purpose and how we want to accomplish it. We do it to model the constructive culture and develop leaders throughout the organization.

If our goal is to develop rather than direct, what types of questions do we ask? In addition, when do we ask questions rather than just do the work?

Let's address the second question first – when do we ask questions? The answer is straight forward – we ask them when there is a need for direction. If the process is flowing smoothly, and the team is working well – let it flow, do the work. If, however, there is a bottleneck, a disruption in the flow, it is time for leadership to help the team identify and correct the underlying issues.

In the classic leadership model, the process may come to a halt waiting for "management" to address the issue. In the pervasive leadership model, individuals within the group will seek resolution. In most cases it involves asking questions and then working together to provide answers. What type of questions?

- What is our goal? What are we trying to achieve?
- How should this work? What are the key steps or elements that must be accomplished to achieve the desired outcome?
- How can we define the challenge, not in terms of who made a mistake, but in terms of what actually happened vs. what was desired and expected?
- Is our problem a result of not implementing the plan as intended or is the process itself weak, not

accounting for all important steps or attributes?

- What were the causes – not just the direct cause, but those hidden contributors that were lurking below the surface?

- Who else should we involve in the solution – what additional skill or experience do we need?

- What could I do to avoid or resolve this problem? What can we do collectively?

- How can we improve our effectiveness? How can we make our job more rewarding?

- What can we learn and apply to the future?

The purpose is to properly focus on the challenge – to constructively seek to define the issue, its underlying causes and, most important, solutions. It is to draw others into the discussion and resolution. In doing so, we gain understanding and commitment. We help develop the constructive culture and build the picture of success. We encourage leadership in others by seeking their insights and respecting their views.

Lastly, there is the question of courage. We often think of the battlefield hero who risks his life to save another. Yes, that is true courage, but so is moving out of our comfort zone to build a stronger, more effective organization. It takes courage to:

- Understand my role and take joy in doing it well by understanding how it fits into our team's overall purpose.

- Challenge the status quo when we see a better way.

- Focus on solving problems rather than assigning blame.

- Encourage someone who is struggling – offering tangible support.

- Embrace other views and feedback concerning our personal performance.

- Develop new skills and adopt new approaches to enhance the team's performance.

- Maintain our team values while not being closed to different views.

- Welcome the idea that my paradigm is incorrect or incomplete and encourage development and implementation of a better approach.

Developing pervasive leadership is not easy. I trust that you will accept the challenge. I did and found life much richer as a result - even as I continue that quest in this journey we call life.

Application: Closing – or is it the Beginning

1. Reflect on a recent team success. What made it successful? How were the Seven Characteristics of Successful Organizations manifested?

2. Review the notes you developed over the course of this book. What are your three most significant leadership strengths? What are the two areas that warrant additional development?

3. Define one leadership attribute that you want to master. Develop a true plan for achieving your goal including specific actions, schedules and accountability for mastering this skill.

"Finally, brothers, whatever is true, whatever is honorable, whatever is just, whatever is pure, whatever is lovely, whatever is commendable, if there is any excellence, if there is anything worthy of praise, think about these things."

Philippians 4:8 ESV

ABOUT THE AUTHORS

Bryce L. Shriver, Ph.D., MBA, MS, BS

Bryce Shriver enjoyed a 40 year career in the nuclear power industry, starting as a nuclear engineer in the U.S. Navy and later serving on the engineering faculty at the University of Virginia. After transitioning to the electric utility business, he became a senior executive before retiring from that role in 2008. Since 2008 Bryce has been actively involved in leadership consulting around the world as the primary face of Three-Seven Research, Inc.

Bryan S. Shriver, BS

Bryan Shriver has enjoyed a varied career starting as a newspaper editor and currently serving as Vice President of Information Technology for a credit union. He is responsible for gaining the benefits of advanced technology in the financial industry. Bryan offers unique perspectives on leadership and technology.

Brandon B. Shriver, MS, BS

Brandon Shriver is the youngest member of Three-Seven Research, but has a broad range of experience in the heavy truck industry starting as a test engineer at an independent facility and a manufacturing engineer for a leading Class 8 Truck manufacturer both before graduating from college in 2008. Since 2008 Brandon worked as a test engineer, and now works as a Product Structure Specialist providing oversight in the design process. Brandon also serves on the board of directors for a local children's museum.

ABOUT THREE-SEVEN RESEARCH, INC

Three-Seven Research was incorporated in 2004 to improve organizational performance through development and application of innovative leadership approaches.

"Applying innovation and the timeless principles of the first century to build a better twenty-first century"

The name, Three-Seven Research refers to the three primary roles of the leader (to create the future, develop a positive culture, and deliver exceptional results) and the Seven Characteristics of Successful Organizations (p15).

The name also represents our spiritual heritage, Three representing the Holy Trinity and Seven representing completeness.

"Wisdom has built her house, she has hewn out her seven pillars."

Proverbs 9:1 NKJV

The book cover pictures a sailing ship. Its three masts and seven sails are an appropriate symbol for this Three Seven Research, Inc. concept paper. The ship captures the energy that surrounds it, compelling it to provide a useful purpose. That is the foundational principle of "pervasive leadership" – the capturing of the existing talent and energy of organizations to benefit society.

Made in the USA
Middletown, DE
07 January 2018